The Makings of This Woman

Myrna Richter

AOS PUBLISHING, 2023
AOS POETRY, 2023

ISBN: 978-1-990496-15-8
Cover Design: Myrna Richter

Visit AOS Publishing's website:
www.aospublishing.com

To my younger self.
I'm sorry you were always afraid,
I will do better for you.

They are easily disillusioned and then they are angry
with you, for it was the illusion they loved.
– W. Somerset Maugham

The Makings of This Woman is a dream coming to fruition. I have aspired to put a poetry book together for as long as I can remember but fear always held me back.

Writing my feelings in poetic form has always come naturally to me and I have found a great deal of comfort in this type of expression. While I understand that my earliest poems are juvenile at best, they are indeed a true reflection of the writer who wrote them; a juvenile herself. A girl with a thousand thoughts and a desperate need for an outlet. Poetry became that outlet, and in the years to come I have always come back to it when I've needed to release the thoughts roaming around inside of me.

I have been inspired by many poetic artists throughout my journey as a poet. Memories of reciting Robert W. Service's "The Cremation of Sam Magee" aloud to myself at the age of twelve, and of being mesmerized by Christina Rosetti's "Remember" were only the beginning for me. As I grew into my later teenage years, the American poet and singer/songwriter Jim Morrison became my biggest inspiration during this period. My adult years have been filled with the words of Margaret Atwood, Leonard Cohen, and Charles Bukowski. As my poetic influences and admirations change and remold themselves, just as I myself have been remolded through the years, through aging and through the experience of life, their words always linger somewhere inside.

Divided into four sections, The Makings of the Woman is a collection of poetry I have written as a young girl, a young adult, and as a middle-aged woman. While the pieces in this collection are not all perfectly refined in style, diction, and maturity, they are a true representation and collection of my mind at the time they were written.
This is who I once was, and this is who I am still.

The Words of Youth
Part One

Every day I wonder what I should feel
Maybe full of life or full of sorrow
Never really knowing what is real
Or even if I can face tomorrow
Some days smiles are all that are shown
Sometimes they are real, sometimes they are fake
Some days my happiness is unknown
And I'm smiling for someone else's sake
There are days when my eyes are drowned in tears
Not once do they get a chance to look straight
Flooded for reasons of worry or fear
Of just what lies ahead for me, my fate
And on the days when I don't know what to say
Give me a hug and tell me it's okay

- Turning feelings into words at age fourteen

My mother's child dances in the rain when no one is home
My mother's child cries desperate tears to a dozen empty chairs
My mother's child rages out in shame and fear as she sits in the dark of her room
My mother's child is afraid, cold, and blind
She is scared of being forgotten
My mother's child is lonely, her heart leaks the dry dust of a fool

Yes, she's a fool

My mother's child's eyes tell a million stories, some of which are true
My mother's child is weak and crazy, her mind and thoughts confuse her heart's wants
My mother's child is never satisfied, always looking for something/someone better
My mother's child, who is she?
Is she the GIRL they all love to tease, bug, joke with, and touch?

NO!

My mother's child is the girl who goes home depressed and angry,
always wondering what she did wrong
My mother's child is stabbed with jealousy, she wants it all
She wants to be the princess, the tomboy, the whore, the freak, the plain Jane
My mother's child, the girl they love to hate

Yes, she's a snob and a flirt

But underneath all the words and thoughts
My mother's child wants to be loved

- My fifteen-year-old heart finally speaks

Her voice cries to the wind
The wind cares not
The wind blows on
She moans silently, softly
No one hears
But the voices rambling inside her
So much pain she carries
So much anger
So much loss
Love she finds, but she is still scared in her frail, bruised heart
She is longing to cry real tears
But her eyes remain dry and tired
It's all building up inside her
She can't take it anymore
She's ready to burst, to scream to the world
"I hurt so bad and no one notices. I need help."
Still, it's only the wind that hears
And it, too, simply moves on

- Words locked inside a young mind

If I could grow wings out my back and turn myself inside out
I'd fly away from this aching pain I feel
Fly away from my newfound emptiness
And all the things that could hurt me
I'd fly away from my life

I wish I was a butterfly

I'd use the strength I do not have
And leave my loneliness behind
I'd wrap myself in a cocoon and sleep away
My guilt, my shame, my anger
I'd sleep away the time I'm dreading
The time I am forced to live without you
My never-ending year of loneliness

I wish I was a butterfly

No food would I need to survive
I'd live off my love for you
I'd try to rebuild my dying soul with the love you gave
I'd fly to your new world, like the angel I never knew I was or could be

If I could only be a butterfly

- Surviving young love

Searching for Survival
Part Two

I AM ALONE

—
I AM ALONE
believe
I AM ALONE

Though I have my peers
Knowing faces
Even my love
I AM ALONE

Give me peace, but not lonely peace
Give me faith, but not questionable faith
Give me strength, but not outer strength
I AM ALONE

Forgive me for I am unknowing
Forget that I have made mistakes
Pretend that I am not a fool
I AM ALONE

If you could see me
Feel me
Love me
Begin to understand me
Then maybe one day I could say
I AM NOT ALONE
ANYMORE
believe
I AM NOT ALONE

Until then I will whisper to the person who isn't listening
I AM ALONE

I've fallen in love so many times,
Over and over and over
It's an obsession
A compulsive disillusion
And in turn my heart is broken
Over and over and over
Every time I create a fabrication love
Between you, anonymous you, and me
I need you
I want you
Like an addiction
The passion is my high
Your soul is my bottle
And I created the situation
And I created the misunderstanding
And I will make you love me
To get my fix
It's messed up, I know
But I can't stop
On and on I go
Falling for you
Falling in love
Falling further from heaven

- Faceless loves

And for you
I lay down my face
and cried a thousand tears

And for you
I let my blood spill over my skin
and let the scars shine bright

And for you
I let my mind run free
while my body remained in chains

And for you
I gave away my heart
and never had it returned
even when you
didn't want it either

And for you
I gave away my body
while you gave me demands

And for you
I risked it all
and you simply hung me out to dry

And for you
I gave everything
And you gave me silence

- On giving too much away

I need this melancholy
To help me write

I need this desperation
To make me sing

I need this mystery
To have something to say

All this brutality and pain
And anger and regret
All the times I fucked up
And all the things I did and did not do
To make myself feel any sort of real feelings

I am tired
So tired of hiding it all
Because I am sick of this charade
Being this phony face
I'm the illusions they wanted me to be
Trapped in the fictitious world I helped to create

I am the creator
I am the destroyer
Of all this reality that isn't real
I will wake up and have nothing but these words

- The hopeless twenty-something

And I swore that I would love you for as long as I lived
I was not lying
And how this love I have for you eats away my insides
And tears away at my heart
It's collapsing inside me
I don't have to love you anymore
And yet I do –
How many suns have passed
Since I saw you last
A stranger's face I will never forget
Those who promise to love forever
Be sure to know that once promised it might never let
you go
A greedy oath to be sure
A prayer sent out to God to make us forever
Well He's holding me to it
As I lie here loving you
I'm lying here without you
Knowing that I left you

- On failing to let go

My fire is dying
Water bombed by failure and unrewarded effort
Mediocrity
The loss of love
The end of triumph
Pushed off my pedestal
Where I'd sat for only a moment

Smoke billows with visions of unchosen paths
Floating upwards to sky carrying away all my limited
potential
With its final puffs and grey swirls
In its final breaths
It gasps with hidden laughter
It's mocking me now
Leaving only stinky ashes behind
On the dirty ground
Where I am not good enough to tread
Anymore

Its greatness is more than my worth
Not perfection
Never perfection
Never to reach the heat, the glow, the power of the
embers
Never to reach what I was never destined to become
My fire is dying
I am unmoved

- Alone in university hallways

The words I write upon the page

Risk being construed in the wrong way
Risk being construed in the right way

Would you know this is written for you?
Would the lingering pain flow between each line?
Would the scent of regret rise up from the page?
Would the message of love be felt in time?
Would you understand this better if it were to rhyme?

These words are just words
These words are just *my* words

And if I write them
And if you read them
There is no middle ground for denial
Anymore

-The denial factor

Finding My Footing
Finding My Voice
Part Three

Peering into the cold, damp forest
Luscious and mysterious
Terrifying and thrilling

Wondering if you should enter
Knowing the warm, sun-kissed field beckons
you back from whence you came
Fear picks your brain
Desire tickles your heart
Restlessness gnaws on your flesh

Conformity and authenticity
Propriety and misdeeds
Salvation and condemnation

Before you an uncertain truth
Behind you a certain death

The earth below reminds you of what you're made of
And the wind teases you with what you could become

Grab your ax, my love
We're going in

- On change and courage

I am not one thing
I am everything
Tiny tidbits of shattered grace
Ancestral spirits ready to take their place

I am not one thing
I am everything
Tattered traces of torn tragedy
Burdened by their apparent apathy

I am not one thing
I am everything
The dark and the light
The day and the night

I am not one thing
I am everything
And because I am everything
I can do anything

- Opening my eyes

My feet are caught
Twisted in thorn-covered vines
Made of promises and lies
Made of wicked judgments
Made of falsified cries

The knots are tight
The vines are long
Survival is questionable
My keeper is strong

I thought I might escape
If I tried to wiggle a bit more
But I thwarted my own efforts
Because I'm a self-saboteur at the very core

So no, I did not succeed
In this self-emancipation
Though my involvement will be denied
I was the vine that caused my downfall
That I, myself, had tied

- Self sabotage

FIDDLE-DEE-DEE

—

Eve ate the apple and it was silky sweet
But Adam held the pen and signed Eve's defeat
For tales are told by the winners that be
Not by losers, heathens, or by me
What voice do I have, but one that's too meek?
It isn't puny arms, but pronouns that make me weak
'She' and 'Her' come with great lessons to be taught
Couplet after couplet my rhythm has been caught
You can see by my words no wit have I
Anything more complicated should be presumed a lie
But what would you expect from just a girl?
Besides a silly song or dance with a twirl
A sweet little thing full of silly malarkey
Thank you, kind Sir, and thank you Patriarchy

...But what if...

If my words weren't so kind?
If I said what was really on my mind?
So bored of your stories and all the little fables
Time we got up from these masochistic tables
Like a little birdie filled with anger and filled with rage
Fuck the bird and the fuck the cage
Words that upset the kin and disembowel the house
I'd rather be the witch than the quiet little mouse
Step out of the shadows and shake off our scorn
Time for You, and Me, and Eve to be reborn

UNBOUND

—
Stop and listen
Voices from the shadows, somewhere in the distance
Their wildness from the past
>   Grasping
>   Pulsating
>   Fighting to be heard
Wanting to break these chains at last
My mind holds their faces, though my eyes have never
seen them
The weight of their grief on my shoulders
Holy burdens burn in my heart
Their stories linger in my throat
I try to cough, but they are not my secrets to tell
Who are these haunting strangers that I know all too
well?
You've probably felt them in your own wilderness
In your dreams or maybe your nightmares
A paradox of
>   Pain and pleasure
>   Fear and freedom
>   Sin and savior
Where does it end if you don't know where to begin?
Like a warrior who weeps her silent cries and wipes dry
tears from her face
Is it her or me or you?
We are tied together by leather ropes disguised as lace
Can we loosen this knot?
A complicated emancipation of the past and the future
She is the key and she is the lock

In the great blaze of the dawn or the perfect stillness of
night
They will be there to
>Greet us
>Meet us
>Teach us
Located somewhere in the middle
Where savage meets grace
The truth is out there
Waiting to be found
No longer a broken feminine soul
But rather a wild spirit unbound
It's time

SUNDAY DRIVE

—

A carcass on the road
I steer the car around it
Gnawed ribs arch towards the sky
And its eyes still glisten in the sun
There is nothing behind the sparkle
I direct the children's attention
To the other side of the road
It's easier this way
The eyes of babes are tender
Some things can't be unseen
I know this all too well
I see it almost every day
The decay of a life left unlived
I pull the wheel in my embrace
The only control I have
The tires maneuver around the wormy lump
A slight puff of dust in sight
Leaves brief evidence of my being
A magpie perched on its decomposing throne
Hardly moves from its feast
Only enough to acknowledge my dissonance
But offers no consolation
I step on the gas
In a rush to leave
The gritty gravel flies wildly free
With unwarranted panic

When we meet in Paris
We shall stroll along the cobbled streets
As real lovers would
I'll wear a yellow dress
And you will smoke a sweet-spiced pipe
Our hands embraced as we walk
(We will never mention how time has ~~aged~~ forsaken us both)
We'll feast upon the crumbs left behind from true lovers
And pretend it's simply a delicacy we cannot pronounce
This will make us giggle
And sneak young lovers' kisses
(Like we used to, like we cannot do)
The rotting rancid grapes become our wine
And we'll toast to days never to come
Let us get drunk on our rank drinks
Making us recite our poetry and make love through the night
(The wine pairs well with this phantasmal romance)

- Fictional memories

29

I lost my friend to God
And now I am without
I can do my best to be kind
But I think we both know
I can't turn this water into wine

Or perhaps I can show you my wrath
Through fierce fire and brimstone
Now, that's something to be feared
But I think we both know
I can't pull off that beard

So the next time I cross your mind
Even if the moment is fleeting
Say a prayer for me
Because I lost my friend to God
And I can't compete with thee

- God : 1, Me : 0

Because it's two in the morning and I cannot sleep
I think back to you and the secrets we keep
And on the pillow, I can still smell your hair
But my rational insides know it's better that you are not there
For you are a beautiful beast in so many ways
You covet my nights and defile my days
We can not
Will not
Shall not
Make a mockery of everything that is pure and good
Only to make our saddened souls feel understood
No
Our demons cannot collide anymore
For we are like a shining bright apple
That is rancid and rotten to its very core

- On toxic unity

There was something simple and sad about the way
She ran her fingers over the printed worlds

Words of love and lust
Words of tears and tiny deaths

She wondered if he wrote them for her
She wondered if he thought about her at all

It wasn't enough to know he was out there breathing
It wasn't enough to have once known every inch of his being

It was an ache that she could not explain
It was an ache she could not control

The longing was her constant companion
The longing was her steady survival

- Surviving longing

I write these words to intrigue you
My dear reader
Of tales of love and passion
Fables of the flesh
Tiny tidbits of a life unlived

A collection of lovers' kisses
On my neck
On my wrists
On my breasts
But the skin is left dry by invisible lips

The pursuit of vivacious carnality
And the search of pleasure
Stripped bare of everything we pragmatically hold dear
Heavy breaths and touches from unruly hands
Leaves the skin of back sand thighs unmarked

These tears fall easily
When they bear no water weight
The breaking, tormenting, smashing of hearts
And the deep longing of tiny deaths
Are easier to endure when there is no blood to spill

The illusion of my words
Hoping to tempt you at best
Turning my mythic moxie
Into a fantasy looping in your mind
And the story has found a place to occupy

- The poet, the squatter

How can I be the whole person
You wanted me to be
When you only loved half my offering?
A flesh debt paid in full
But you left me to spoil in vain
Because it amused you to watch me gag
On the rank rancid rot you proclaimed
Was not good enough
Was not pretty enough
Was not grateful enough
To be served on a silver platter
And devoured at your kingly feast

- Flesh and other debts

I glorified your starvation
And the slow death of your youthful greens
Those are the days I want to remember
And yet I can't quite seem to stop watching you die
Some may say it's simply transitional
A time for rest and rebirth
Like those goddamn seasons of life
We romanticize, fictionalize, Hallmark-icize
But your corpse says otherwise
Sickly, Sullenly, Seriously
Dead inside

- Midlife death hold

You can call me Bethany
under the moonlight
if it pleases you so
I'd rather be a version
of that yellowed silhouette
than the version of the person
I was before

So you can call me what you'd like
And I can be that girl for you
You can dress me up in silks
That hide my scars
And you can twirl me under the stars
That hold all our secrets

You can feed me grapes
rancid and rank
and I'll pretend it's the sweetest wine
I've ever tasted
You can tell me your lies
While you kiss my thighs
and I won't tell you no
Because the truth is
the version of the person
I am with you
Is the person I wish they all knew
Then maybe love
would follow too

- On being someone

I can write my words in a permanent ink
I can speak my words to you
I can break this typewriter with forceful pounding
But that is not going to make this anymore true

It doesn't really matter what I write
Since it probably won't be read by your eyes
And even if I added a nice rhythm and rhyme
Wouldn't negate the fact that this is merely a collection
of lies

I could pretend to be brilliant and peddle my smut
Glorifying you or God as my chosen muse
Only taking what I want and giving nothing in return
I'd be better off looking for salvation from these broken-
down pews

I am not a writer or a poet
Or even some watered-down version
I am not what you think you read
I am barely a person

How can I proclaim myself to be such a thing?
Giving myself titles reserved for people of credible rank
Like Cohen or Kerouac, Thomas or Whitman
I am no Jack and I am no goddamn Cohen
I am not your man

- Je suis

Modern Micro Thoughts
Part Four

Every part of me wants to believe
That the moon could shine without the sun
And I could shine without you
And we'd both still be lovely

I am tired of trying to be everything
I am not
I am tired of hiding everything
I am

I am not nearly perfect
I am mostly tragic
I am not blandly ordinary
I am ridiculously magic

She left the remnants of magic
Wherever she had been
With the scent of Chanel
And the taste of sin

When I stop mourning the loss
Of a conditional normal
I start to see the sparkle
Of a bewildering abnormal

It wasn't the touch of his hand
that made her pause
Or how his skin felt
like well worn satin
It was the force of
two stars finally aligning
Despite being told
they were merely meteors

I was finally free
You had untied me
Then you stopped watching
Before too long
So, I sullenly crept over
And put my collar back on

It's not glitter we leave behind when we walk away
We are not goddamn fairies
It's the glass we are shaking out of our hair

Champagne makes me
remember you
More champagne
makes me miss you
All the champagne
makes me forget you

She was little but sweet
But mostly she was sour
And downright sinister
Upon the midnight hour

I'm sorry, but I have to go
I loved you more than you'll ever know
Wait
Did you just crush my soul with a couplet?
That's some cold shit

To resist sliding my hand along the nape of your neck
Trusts a tantalizing torture
And
Leaves my soul in a wreck

Somewhere between here and there
You and me
Lies that wretched middle ground
Where we are not quite strangers
Not quite lovers
But simply souls
Screaming a muted intimacy
Silenced by the constructs in which we are bound

Our passion was greater than we
Ever let on
Ever let be shown
Ever let be known
Even to ourselves

Denial is a beautiful thing
Denial is a damaging thing

The storm had a fury that not even
Mother Nature could contain
For you were the thunder
And I was the rain

I wanted to look up at the stars with you
But this sky was too cloudy
And you are someone I only once knew

The goose bumps on your skin
Tell me more secrets than the
Heart that won't let me in

Cheers to those....

Who fall in love too soon
Who fall in love with the moon
Who ate the ice cream and wanted more
Who look for hope from pennies found on the floor
Who carry their heavy hearts full of secret places
That hold a lifetime of moments with forgotten faces

He tastes like
Ill intentions
Hurting Hearts
Titillating Torture

And I am famished

You tickled my tongue
Like sparkling champagne
And left me hungover just the same

The distance between each star
In the night's sky
Is where I hide my love for you

The spark drew me in
Your flame was more smoke than fire
I choked on the soot

The silly secrets we carry
Like skinny dipping in the dark
Stealing kisses in the light
Basking in the waves of sin
All while pretending to be affrighted

I was afraid to show my true colours
Because you only fancied beige

Not made from riblets
But devoured just the same
My Lilith – My Jane

After I resisted
I became human

I write so I can breathe
I write so I can see
I write to be free
I write for me

I was conditioned to believe.......
My worth was based on your approval
My happiness was based on your restrictive love
My intelligence was based on your understanding

+

I was destined to become........
A creative being who dreams in neon
A lover of language, words, and sounds
A reckless spirit with a burning passion

=

A brilliantly beautiful mess